# EVIDENCE FOR GOD

# EVIDENCE
# FOR
# GOD

*by*

Edmund Flood

PAULIST PRESS
New York / Paramus / Toronto

Library of Congress
Catalog Card Number 72-91455

ISBN 0-8091-1741-X

Published by Paulist Press
*Editorial Office:* 1865 Broadway, N.Y., N.Y. 10023
*Business Office:* 400 Sette Dr., Paramus, N.J. 07652

Printed and bound in the
United States of America

# Contents

# I
# Whom Are We
# Talking About?

It's useful to start from the simplest possible point. So let us just take what most people understand by "God," and let us leave aside for the moment the question whether he exists.

Now when we talk about God I think we mean, very roughly, (1) a power who is supreme over all other powers, and (2) a power that is personal.

From this elementary perception we can advance a long way. But before going on, we should just glance at a hazard which can halt all development and which is a permanent threat to any venture of this kind.

For what happens, if we're not careful, is that we stick to the merely physical. An example would be the assertion that God is supreme. Doesn't this immediately suggest height? So we visualize God as being *above* everyone.

Granted we're not to blame for that. It's how our imaginations work. But what we're not forced

1

to do is to stop there. Maybe we have to *imagine* supremacy, but we can also *think through* to what it means. What I'm saying here is that when we constantly keep this hazard in mind we will, unaware, neglect the thinking stage. The whole of this book will reinforce the obvious truth that God is principally met through a response of the *whole* person, in which thought is indispensable.

With this danger in mind, then, let us consider our starting point: God, if he exists, has supreme power, and is personal.

If we restrain ourselves from imagining power as just physical, we realize that the more important kind of power is personal, and hence supreme power must above all be personal. So we'd better consider the personal: in other words ourselves.

## God as Personal

Now whereas I develop myself physically by eating and exercise, I become more of a person through my personal relationships. Even these we can slide into considering at a merely physical level. In fact the crucial decision in any attempt to know God is to move toward an awareness of *personal* relationships. Let us make this attempt now.

A "relationship" between two persons sounds like A linking up with B; and no harm need be done by imagining it in that way if we consider what this "link" consists of. But we must bear in mind that here we are trying to penetrate to what our lives are: to our human nature at its deepest. So it can't be all that easy.

An example will help, so we'll take marriage. A husband and wife live in the same house, probably see each other for some hours each day, sleep together, and know each other's characteristics with considerable thoroughness. Yet all these things don't *necessarily* mean that there is a personal relationship between the two people concerned. Many a broken marriage had all of them, but lacked the one thing that was necessary.

But a marriage can also, of course, show us when there is a real personal relationship. Jane, for example, feels that Bill, her husband, loves her *not* merely because he is good-humored and generous toward her but because she feels *he is alongside her in what she is trying to do:* to give their children a good upbringing, to make the home pleasant for him, and to develop her other talents when she has time. She feels he is entering into her life, which means basically how she sees, and is trying to see more clearly, her responsibilities, opportunities and so on. He's really in on it all with her: sympathetic about the snags and failures, amused at the odd occurrences it throws up, glad at the achievements. Where a husband and wife share that kind of attitude toward each other, we have love. Without that kind of attitude, can we really call it a *personal* relationship at all?

It's the same of course with any other kind of

personal relationship. It means a warm, sympathetic sharing in the other person's purposes.

After all it is *purposes* that define a person: that make him what he is. A moment ago we listed Jane's main purposes (for her children, the home, her talents). Of course she'll have hundreds of smaller purposes, from a new pair of gloves to being kinder to that unpleasant neighbor. More important, though, even her main purposes *will be developing*. It's easy enough to decide to give the children a good upbringing but not so easy to decide what that is. So this is a problem she'll have to wrestle with while the children become older and the world they're living in changes. And she'll feel that Bill is really close to her insofar as he comes in on this with her: not as a law-giver or oracle (though she'll be glad of his advice), or as a mere observer, however sympathetic, but as a *partner* who shares in all the effort, celebrations, joys, monotony and worries of the developing enterprise, this great venture, on which she has set her heart and which she knows is a means of her becoming herself.

When we look like this at an example of either the absence or the presence of a personal relationship, it is easy for us to see what it consists of. Naturally such a subtle and profound thing is much easier to see than to define. A rough definition might be *a sharing in the quest for meaning*.

I know that sounds rather nebulous. Why "meaning" particularly? Well let's look again at Jane's wanting to give her children a good upbringing. Unless (as is possible) she's ceased to be a person and merely become a machine, she won't simply get her idea of a good upbringing out of a book. She's always in search of a better understanding of what it involves. And what will basically guide her in her search will be how she understands, however implicitly, what a person is for, what the contemporary world is like, and how her children should best be adapted to it. In other words she is always exploring this complex pattern and seeking for what is of real *human* value in it: in short, its significance of meaning. Obviously she can fail to make that quest (and which of us makes it completely?). She can just follow a line that comes easiest. But so far as she is *human,* she will be seeking for the human value, for the meaning in the light of what really counts and of the whole. And a personal relationship with her will be the sharing in that quest for meaning, for it is in that that she is most a person.

At this point let us see where we've got to. First we reminded ourselves of what we understand by "God"—whether or not we believe he exists. He is the supreme power and personal. We then tried to establish a permanent warning signal to alert us to the fact that at every stage we can slide into a merely physical conception of God: as supreme, as powerful, as personal, or whatever.

We then tried to see what we mean by the personal. Here we turned to ordinary human experience.

We saw that we become persons insofar as we seek to work out the human significance of things, and a personal relationship is an intimate and warm sharing in this quest for meaning. With this established, we are now in a position to realize what we mean by calling God personal. What will help us in doing this is looking at the same time at "God," meaning also the supreme power.

## God as the Supreme Power

Power, we saw, must be personal, not just physical. So it must be to do with the quest for human significance or value that the personal is all about. Power is entering into that quest effectively and personally. A parent or a school teacher is likely to have more power than the man with the biggest engine.

Once we see this, we can understand God much better. God's power is in helping us work out the meaning of our lives: helping us, in other words, to become persons. Of course, being "supreme," it is of a very special kind. It will be especially *personal:* in its warmth, delight, intimacy, understanding. In this it will be true to us as we really are. And it will be true to us, too, in another respect that we haven't yet considered. This is that we are part of something greater than ourselves. We belong to mankind and find ourselves, as individuals, in committing

6

ourselves to man's service. God, then, is essentially the sharer with us in this great enterprise of becoming a person, in its full width and creative zest.

To say this is to say nothing new or elaborate. All we have done is to resist the merely physical view of God and to see what is *really* involved in any man's ordinary understanding of God.

But though it's all very ordinary, it also points toward wonderful perceptions of God and of ourselves.

First, to the intimacy of God. Because we can't see and touch God, we easily imagine him as remote. But physical contact doesn't constitute personal intimacy. Persons are intimate in the way we saw: when they share this working out of meaning. This is the true union of mind and will and sympathy: a mutual penetration of personalities, so that each may be enriched, more fruitful.

Then, it points also to the creativity of God. Here again we can think, if we don't take care, merely of the physical: atoms and the rest. But if we keep to the personal, we see that creativity is what personal life is all about. Jane, if I may come back to her, doesn't work long hours for her children's upbringing because of some preconceived moral plan (though such a plan could help her see things more clearly). But her actual motive is that she wants to *make* something: to "make" men and women out of her children.

She knows she's working with the most wonderful "material" going: people. People with their possibilities of a true and generous response to life. She is forming human life, which is the greatest thing we know. And it is in that making something human that she finds human fulfillment.

This is any person's chief kind of creativity: creativity with persons: bringing the *personal* to life, to development: giving reality to the ultimate richness of life.

God, therefore, must, if he exists, be more closely, more purposefully, more delightedly involved in this kind of creativity than anyone. In fact it must be his main activity, his main presence, in the world. Involvement with persons is the hallmark of his nature.

# II
# Evidence for the Christian God

Anyone would agree, I suppose, that the God we have been considering would, if he exists, be overwhelmingly attractive and relevant. But does he exist? Haven't you merely taken the gaps in life of purposelessness, moral evil, suffering and death and merely papered them across with a product of wishful thinking?

Now there are, it seems to me, two ways in which this question should be answered. But each way is incomplete without the other, for reasons I shall suggest.

## EVIDENCE FROM OUR NEED FOR GOD

The first way is to take the miseries or the contingency of life; to point to how irrational these strike us as being when we really face up to them; to remind ourselves that all our human actions, from the greatest discovery of research to driving a car, are based on everything being by nature rational; and by deducing from this, by various stages of argument, that there is a God.

I am not concerned to dispute that this *can* be an effective line of argument—I've merely given a very rough summary. But in practice it is for most people too much tied up with logic and ideas to produce more than a pale, intellectual "God" at the end. The personal, which is the very center of God's nature, tends in practice to get left out; and all we are left with is a *thing,* a missing link, that ties the apparently irrational into the neatly rational.

Since this book is not designed for the specialist in philosophy, I shall therefore concentrate on the second way. But before we come to it a further word must be said about the way just mentioned.

This is that for all of us it is *in one respect* indispensable. As *proof,* it can be neglected. But as making us aware of our absolutely fundamental *need* for God, it cannot be dispensed with. It reminds us that the deepest realities of our nature cry out for a God and hence prevents us from regarding him as a merely interesting extra whom we may occasionally care to heed. True, we have not yet asked ourselves whether there *is* a God to give an answer to that cry. But at least we know what we are talking about when we do ask that question, and to it we now turn.

Christianity is about a God; and so is the Hebrew religion from which it sprang. But is the God of which they spoke credible today? And if he is, is he important for the lives we lead? How, for instance, could we possibly believe in the angry God of the Old Testament? And does even the God of the New Testament come over to us as convincing and relevant?

I believe that the God of which the Old and New Testaments speak is not merely credible but true. The more we look at the evidence, and the closer we get to the experience these books portray through the researches of scholars, the more poignantly real does this God become.

I shall now offer some evidence for this view, taking the New Testament as offering the clearest. In a book of this size, I need hardly say, we shall have to be selective, not exhaustive!


## EVIDENCE FROM THE NEW TESTAMENT

### The Basic Message

What is the New Testament about? What basically is it saying to us?

St. Paul does more than *give* an answer to this question: he *presupposes* the answer he mentions as already accepted by his correspondents, the Corinthians. In fact so firmly rooted does he think it must be in them that he uses it as a basis to prove a most unpopular (to the Corinthians) doctrine that ran

11

counter to their most cherished feelings. "Christ raised from the dead is our message," he says.

It was the same with Peter. Like Paul he always stressed that the business of his life was to lay before people not a theory but a fact. He was not a philosopher but a witness. He had seen something which he felt it was vital that everyone should know about. So the explanation he gave of what he was doing, to the Jerusalem crowd in the first days after Christ's death, was: "You killed the prince of life. *But God raised him from the dead*. And to that fact we are the witnesses" (Acts 3:15).

But what has this got for us? Since it was presented as *the Good News* for every man and woman, we must ask this question.

The difficulty here is not in searching out an answer but to select which aspect of the answer to start from. The reason is that *the whole New Testament reflects the answer*. For the point of that book was to reflect the life of a diverse, far-flung community whose purpose it was to live out that answer: by reflection, by action, in all the manifold business of life and death, friendship and dispute, joy and sorrow: to live out the effect of Christ having risen from the dead.

We must therefore *choose* one of many possible starting points, and a good one would be the message of Christ before his death.

## Jesus in Palestine

His message was that now that he, Jesus of Nazareth, was here, God had come to rule fully in this world (the meaning of "the kingdom of God," where "kingdom" should really read "rule").

Now "rule" can, of course, mean all kinds of things, but basically it means the effective exercise of power. But power used for what purpose? To get political independence, more territory, an easier life, or what?

Since the message of Jesus hinged on what kind of power this was—in other words, what it aimed to do—both his actions and words were mainly designed to make this as evident as he could. Since it wasn't the crude kind of power that people wanted, his task was, to say the least, difficult.

If you had the eyes to see, what you actually saw and heard from Jesus was a richer kind of human living.

## His Friends

Chiefly, you *saw* it. Since the only account we have of his life is words in a book, we easily forget that, to the people Jesus was working among, his actions were more conspicuous than his words.

There he was, then, a rabbi; one of those people whose job was to go up and down the country instructing people. But this man was glaringly different. The differences from the other members of that sedately respectable profession hit you in the face. Even at that slow-moving time, with its slow communications, these differences set the country on edge in a matter of months and made suppression politically necessary in two years.

The differences were these. First there was the company he kept. It wasn't just that some of his acquaintances were disreputable people. To most of his countrymen they were dirt. They were people that made you want to spit.

Nor was this some freakish animosity, some odd quirk of character that the Jews of that time had somehow contracted. In Northern Ireland, at the time of writing this, Catholic girls who go out with members of "the occupying forces" may be tarred, feathered and tied to lamp-posts. People who consort with "the occupying forces" have always been liable to be hated. And when the "consorting" consists of forcing taxes from their compatriots, on behalf of the occupiers and by often rapacious means, the hatred and contempt can be burning. In fact the moral contempt was so mordant that "tax collector" and "sinner" were seen as equivalent.

With this moral and social riff-raff Jesus freely mixed. And they were more than mere acquaintances. The complaint wasn't that he spoke with them but that he *dined* with them: that he feasted with them, as boon companions, with all the profound social ties that this still sets up in an Eastern country.

This flouting of religious custom can only be understood if taken together with the other main differences seen in Jesus.


## His Impression on People

First came the feel of the man. Even at this distance of time, relying on mere documents, we catch its remarkable quality. He knew what he was about. He spoke of what he knew. He subverted old ways because he had better to give.

There was an astonishing four-squareness about him that made rejection difficult. Mark tells us about it in his first chapter: "The people were so astonished that they started asking each other what it all meant. 'Here is a teaching that is new,' they said, 'and with authority behind it.' "

"We have never seen anything like this," said the crowd at Capernaum as Jesus cured a paralytic; and the same magnetism was felt by the fishermen who gave up everything at the command of a stray and unestablished acquaintance and by the centurion who, though "not of your persuasion," knew authority when he met it.

But what did it all mean? Why was this mixing with moral outcasts, the endless string of cures, and the calm sense of absolute assurance: why was all this to do with the immediate coming of God's rule?

Because they made life different. That they did so and how they did so was the point of the parables to explain.

## His Explanations

A parable is not a way of *telling* your listener something but of encouraging him to see a sudden and fresh perception, like an unexpected window onto a new landscape.

Jesus' parables consider life as his listeners knew it. So there's a God? Yes, but have you understood what that means? See that elderly man who's flung decorum to the winds to run to greet his disgraceful son? See that employer who throws prudence to the winds in offering a day's wages for a couple of hours of work? Yes, those are pictures of the best qualities of a person taken to exuberant, extravagant limits. Well that's the God whose rule I'm bringing. And not in words but actions. In what I do with persons. So isn't it natural that I too should forget decorum in my enthusiasm to forgive: to help those who need it?

Or perhaps you figure another kind of God. The prudent calculator with his eye on the balance sheet? Here's a story, then. A man entrusts money to three slaves, goes off, and on his return asks what they did with it. Two of them had vigorously exploited it. The third, with his mind on a stringent master, had locked it up. Jesus shapes the story, folk-tale-like, to get the contrast he wants: the warm geniality, the almost back-slapping bonhomie of the praise given to the first and the second slave has established the mood. By contrast, the mood of the next bit is icy. It is as hard and hollow as frost. In a different context it would be otherwise. *But the context is the point*. The coming of the rule of God calls for a different kind of world: where rich opportunities are delightedly tossed to you for you to get on with it, and with that kind of welcome when you've finished.

The other stories stressed the opportunity. This full presence of God, this richer relationship with him, isn't something we have but something we live. In fact nothing is really "part of us" unless it comes into the way we live.

So all the stories are about living, about fundamental human attitudes. Not in the form of dry legislation: "do that, and refrain from this." Instead they let us see how those attitudes *feel*. The sense of an intoxicatingly happy discovery, in the treasure and pearl stories. The sense of achievement, as we watch that abundant harvest in the sower story. The sense of utter confidence, whatever the situation, in the story of the unjust judge. And above all the sense of a human person in the Samaritan story.

The Samaritan story is central because it just throws in different form the cause of contention between Jesus and the religious rulers. It shows a man reacting humanly to an enemy. In a world where utter hatred would but intensify with the centuries, this man wrenched himself away from a five-hundred-year-old hostility and saw the beaten-up figure as a man. He responded to him as such and "was moved with compassion when he saw him."

In that simple human action we are in the presence of the kingdom. Isn't that mere humanism, then—to reduce Christianity simply to being human?

## Jesus Brings the Full Presence of God

The answer is, I think, that in the way Christ is presenting this action, this is indeed the kingdom or rule of *God,* and it is therefore *not* a reduction. Since this is crucial to our whole inquiry, I must develop this.

First we must remember that the Samaritan story is only an *illustration.* The man for whose benefit it was told was, like all his countrymen, well aware that what determined whether you were a true member of God's people or not was whether you loved him and your neighbor. So one reasonably went on to ask: "Who is my neighbor?" And it was this question, Luke tells us, that provoked the story.

In fact, by a delicate readjustment, Jesus showed that there was a more important question to be asked, and used his story to answer that. The questioner had thought that the problem lay in which groups one ought to be "neighborly" to; and there was much argument among the Jews at the time about this: fellow Jews, yes; but what about non-Jewish fellow countrymen, was a much-argued question.

Jesus turns the attention from *which category to be neighborly to?* to *what is neighborliness?* Of course the story doesn't define it. It doesn't even tell the questioner what it is. Typically of Jesus, it just helps the questioner *see for himself:* yes, *of course,* it's basically a question of response to the needs and value of a man as he is. I see it clearer now, though I feel I *must* have known something so obvious all the time.

And now we can see what Jesus has done. First it's essential to recognize his starting point. He doesn't start by *asserting* something, but by taking a fundamental insight that is present, however obscurely, in all of us. It's an insight about our personal relationships, and therefore about our lives insofar as they are human.

By responding, like that Samaritan, to the demanding challenge to be human, Jesus is saying we are following the rule of life that the "commandments" map out. But this was said by *Jesus* and *at that particular juncture.* So it wasn't a random commentary, however acute, on the Jewish law, but a presentation of what the full coming of God consists of: people's warm and absolute response to people as they are, just as his was to the tax collectors (in their need of warm acceptance), the sick (in the cures), and the religious rulers and the many who were influenced by them (in his questioning their stunted attitudes).

What Jesus was saying, therefore, was that *God is present* insofar as we become human. The maker is fully present in the full achievement of his work; and if his "work" is persons, the achievement must be gained in their deliberate action. His presence, like any *personal* presence, is in the sharing: whether of the opportunity, the resolution, the success or failure.

But it is the presence of *God*. At his parties with his friends the tax collectors, Jesus would have enjoyed the food and drink. Perhaps he liked the knowledge that, in spite of the scorn he was drawing on himself by the association, his befriending these people was right.

But in and through all this he felt that this action of his, and all his actions, was part of a movement in human affairs that is of total significance. That all he did and all he saw embodied the presence, as of an artist, of a person who could, in his experience, best be called "Father."

It was no part of this recognition that previously there had been none of this. What was new was a far greater opportunity to live in the light of this recognition.

## We Find God in Living

For what Jesus was bringing to light was not something extra to a man's situation, or even just a "behind-the-scenes person." Instead he was bringing to clearer vision how things are. Not the "things" out there, the furniture among which we move and conduct our lives. But the actual business of living.

The presence of your wife, if it is a *real* presence, isn't something you just know about but something you "live." Hence if God is really God, and therefore present wherever life is, all people "live" the presence of God. Most don't see it in those terms. They see a man or woman, perhaps, whom they *must* help. They could hardly tell you why. But they know that if they don't, a warmth will have gone out of life. They will have let something down, though what it is they cannot say.

Nor can we Christians say all that much. How much do we really *understand* our Christian teachings? The center of a Christian's experience is the same as anyone else's: the demand to be human, the sense that otherwise we shall let something down: that something warm and rich—which sometimes we feel could perhaps be *immensely* warm and rich— will have been abandoned, wasted.

Since it is a matter of doing, not saying, the non-Christian can do it better. Often, we know, he does. Often, too, we realize that the Christian lets complacency at his being able to *say* more (invaluable though that *can* be) deflect his attention from the more important sphere of doing.

So our knowledge of God, like that of any person whom we genuinely *know*, comes in our *human* experience.

## Expressions of This in the New Testament

*Human* experience consists of genuine responses to values. It isn't therefore surprising that in the parts of the New Testament where we particularly get the feel of a community sharing a personal life with God, such responses are being expressed.

A clear example is the beginning of the Epistle to the Ephesians. It is an expression of wonder, awe and gratitude at the presence of God in the human situation. It expresses a sense that life has a total significance: conceived through great wisdom, and put into effect with much fruit: "Blessed be God the Father of our Lord Jesus Christ; he chose us in Christ, to live through love in his presence, determining that we should become his adopted sons, through Jesus Christ, for his own kind purposes. . . . Such is the richness of the grace which he showered on us in all wisdom and insight. He has let us know the mystery of his purpose, the hidden plan he so kindly made in Christ from the beginning . . . that he would bring everything together under Christ as head."

It is difficult to miss here the sense of a will shaping in gradual process the totality of life, but graciously, kindly, and in partnership with man, toward fulfillment. The sense, in short, of God.

This experience of this movement toward fulfillment was perhaps the main element of their consciousness of God. Our lives tend to be fragmentary. They lack cohesion and therefore meaning. "Tomorrow and tomorrow and tomorrow creeps in its petty pace from day to day"; and, like Macbeth, we can be contemptuous about the pettiness. What am I to you or you to me, we ask. Who will have heard of me tomorrow?

But a consciousness of God is an awareness that the fragments fall into place. They are taken up into the integrated whole of the one pattern of history, which is the realization of the plan of God among men.

So we get the steady and secure advance in John's Prologue. It is the advance of God throughout history: universal, gentle, and decisive, like the light.

It is also intimate. "The Word became flesh": took for himself, that is, our will-o'-the-wisp condition. But not through a hidden transmutation while no one was aware, for "he lived among us"; we saw him, especially in those qualities of kindness and complete dependability, so that although "no one has ever seen God, it is the only Son who has made him known."

## The Message of Jesus

So far, then, in reflecting on the message of Jesus, we have found it to be something like this.

First of all the message was the man. He had come to offer a way of life, and he showed what it was by living it.

And what the message amounted to was that that elusive hunch, which we sometimes have, and often doubt, is true: that life is as, in our finest moments, we'd have it.

In other words it is personal. This is more than to say that only the persons in the world matter. For the persons in the world, as we know them, are caught up in this drive toward the fragmentary. We find it in the piecemeal quality of our relationships, we find it in our death, and above all we find it in that fundamental self-contradiction in our natures whereby we assert the personal in ourselves by fencing out that of others.

All of these we feel as "wrong," as contradictions of what we are. I must belong to this group and exclude that if I'm to have a recognizable individuality. Even in my belonging to a friend or wife, I must preserve my inner sanctum. I can be a person— a wholehearted sharer in meaning—only by limiting the sharing. And in that sharing itself I need certain categories as guides: he is my neighbor, but not him.

Jesus' message is that this contradiction isn't final. We feel the wrongness of it, we even act on it

—a daring reach into the dark, for we see no clear warrant. The contradiction is resolved because at the heart of life is the completely personal: the full sharing of purpose. In our lives there is God. The close God of the parables, the God whose rule or power is exercised just in our daring reach into the dark, the God of the Christian Ephesians and of John.

To complete this chapter on the New Testament, we need to expand what has been said in two ways. One is to compare the message of Jesus with that of the New Testament. The other is to see how the message is to be lived by Christians.

## The Message of the New Testament: Resurrection

On the first, we have seen that the message of the New Testament is resurrection. This means, of course, the conquering of death. But if we want to understand what this message was trying to say, we must see this victory in its context.

There were a considerable number of ways in which this context was expressed, although, not surprisingly, I suppose, they point to the same thing.

What in general it amounts to is that *the resurrection is the full coming of God to human nature.* And when we look at it more precisely, we find that the point of this coming is to conquer the limitations of our nature.

## Fulfillment versus Futility

This is expressed most obviously in St. Paul's longest consideration of the resurrection. Christ's resurrection means for us that we conquer the contradictions of sin and death. In fact running behind the chapter it is possible to detect an even wider awareness of contradiction. Deliberately placed at the beginning of the Bible are those first lines of Genesis which are meant to introduce us to the *kind* of activity which the history to be recounted will describe. The first line is about chaos: the shapelessness, the "absurd" waste and ruin to which physically and morally—that is, as people—we are liable. And then into this situation comes the shapeful, the meaningful, the wonderful, with the action of God: there is life, and it is "very good." In this chapter St. Paul seems to have in mind the same kind of alternative. The alternative to resurrection, he says again and again, is "futility." The word may even be a reminiscence of the Hebrew word for "chaos" in Genesis. But whether it is or not, St. Paul leaves us in no doubt that he sees resurrection as the completion of God's work of bringing fulfillment to what is liable to absurdity and waste: that his is a quest, exercised through man, for the full implementation of man's meaning.

That this reaches to the whole of creation comes out especially in his Epistle to the Romans. The world, he says in chapter 8 of this letter, is still contaminated with "futility" (the same word is used) and death. But now it is to be freed from this "to enjoy the same freedom and glory as the children of God."

How has this come about? Because something new has entered into the human situation, so that Paul describes the result as a "new creation"—by which he meant a wonderful and ultimate refashioning of the human situation.


## The Coming of God's Power

This entry of "something new" took place fully at the resurrection of Christ: "May he enlighten the eyes of your mind so that you can see what hope his call holds for you . . . and how infinitely great is the power that he has exercised for us believers. This you can tell from the strength of his power at work in Christ, when he used it to raise him from the dead" (Eph. 1:18-20).

We see that Paul calls it the entry of God's "power." Again and again, the resurrection is seen as the exercise of God's "power": the effective presence of God. So outstanding is it, in fact, that in one place Paul refers to Christ simply as "the power of God" (1 Cor. 1:24).

"Power" had for centuries been one of the chief ways in which the Jews had expressed their experience of God as of a person who effectively entered into their situation to achieve its hidden promise, its meaning. Other "gods," they felt, exercised power. But the power exercised by their God was different because it was personal; directed by wise purpose it was supreme; and it was encountered by men in the shaping toward fulfillment of the human situation—in other words, as a fashioning of man's history.

## The Coming of God's Spirit

The resurrection is also seen in terms of the "Spirit," which for the Jews meant the power and presence of God as expansive, inspiring, enabling a man for undreamt of action: the person of God bringing life. It is a personal union whereby we are brought into a sharing in the life-fullness of God: a fullness of understanding, of purpose, of creativity: a total realization of meaning.

It would be quite easy to take other bearings in the New Testament only to arrive at the same goal. This is especially true of "the Word." For John it meant the creative, enlightening power; also Wisdom—the bringing of all things to the harmony of full significance; and this Word "became flesh." "Flesh" meant not the skin over our bones, but ourselves as powerless and liable to meaningless extinction. Once again, then, if we trouble to get beyond the merely physical image and see what in

28

personal terms is being suggested, we come again to the same message: that God has come to join us as intimately as is possible in a total *fulfillment of human meaning.* And lest we think that this is too grand a project for the everyday lives that we lead, Paul shows that genuine *human* living is the very test of God's presence: "What the Spirit brings is ... love, joy, peace, patience, kindness, goodness, truthfulness, gentleness and self-control" (Gal. 5:22), while in Romans he reminds us of the cause and effect of this: "If the Spirit of him who raised Jesus from the dead is living in you, then he who raised Jesus from the dead will give life to your own mortal bodies through his Spirit living in you" (Rom. 8:11).

# III
# God in
# "A Godless World"

We began this book by inquiring what God, if he exists, would be like. We then considered the claim by men and women who lived two thousand years ago that a man they knew was "the radiance of the Father's splendor and the full expression of his being" and that he was born simply to make God fully accessible to all people. Let us suppose for the moment that their claim was true (personally I cannot account otherwise for the evidence). How does their claim affect people in our Western world, for most of whom God is of little significance, if, indeed, they believe in him at all?

To be realistic, we must begin by recognizing that belief (whether in God or in others) is seldom particularly articulate, conscious or coherent. These limitations do not necessarily prevent it from acting profoundly for a lifetime. We see the truth of this in many marriages and in the kind of loyalty many people have to friend, employer or country.

For human life is a matter of *doing,* not so much *in the light of* (which would imply methodical thought) as *impelled* by largely inarticulate perceptions. The fact that these are perceptions of value or meaning, and that we feel that we are becoming our true selves in the way we respond (or don't) to these perceptions, makes us human instead of mechanical.

If the Christian assertion is right that all *human* life ("love") is a living in fellowship with God, a life with God, then this must in practice take place in this not greatly deliberative or even coherent implementation of our meaning that most human life is. A man, for instance, decides to give up a weekend activity to be more with his wife and kids ultimately because he feels, however subconsciously, that he'll be more himself, truer to what he should be realizing in life, by doing so.

Should we call this *belief* in God? Well, first of all this is a secondary question, because obviously the main thing is not belief but life. Also, if you choose to mean by "belief" some rather articulate motivation, then one has to bear in mind that, as we have just seen, human life does not normally operate by rather articulate motivation, and that it *is* human life in which God operates (incarnation, after all!).

But can you have belief in someone if you are not conscious of him and do not know even that he exists?

Before answering this question we must recall what it is that we are conscious of. However obscurely and disjointedly, we are conscious of fulfilling ourselves by helping to implement the goodness in things. In this we find ourselves part of something greater than ourselves; in fact for all the obvious pressures in our society that make us concentrate on the piecemeal (specialization, etc.), we sometimes feel ourselves as part of a whole, which must, since it is of humans, be a common working out of meaning.

In other words we are aware (however dimly) that our lives are personal, and that the "personal" we find there is more than the individual human person. (Of course the extent to which we perceive the quality of that "more"—the possible splendor of the human achievement—obviously varies with the individual.)

Now I have sought to suggest that if by God we mean a supreme person, and if by "person" we mean a sharer in the quest for significant life, it is *only* in the kind of *awareness* just described that God is knowable, because it is precisely in that quest that God is active and present.

But it does not follow that we put the name "God" to our experience. First of all we don't usually put a name to something that we're not very explicitly aware of. It is difficult for us to be explicit about the profoundest realities of our lives (I can tell you distinctly which make of car suits me best, but I'd find it much more difficult to tell you why I love someone). And to decide to put the name "God" to this experience could only come at the end of much explicit reflection on what our experience of the personal ultimately points to and what "God" would mean. Such a reflection, moreover, is a reach into the profoundest depths of our experience, where we find ourselves—if we care to travel much in that direction anyway—traveling down avenues whose end we cannot reach. It would be on a reflection as rare and as exploratory as this that one would put the name "God."

In other civilizations it was much easier to do so. In primitive societies the adult retains what we all start with as children: the awareness of belonging to a whole which is greater than ourselves. A primitive awareness tends, as such, to lack a developed sense of the personal. And hence the particular aspect of this wholeness and greatness which a tribe feels most prominent, and hence most apt for its own involvement in it, may have no very personal traits. In fact I think it is true to say that, apart from the Jewish-Christian God, there is no case of a God who is attributed personality *as God*. Non-Christian gods are given personal traits, as any reader of the Greek or Roman classics knows. But those personal traits, when they are present, make them less gods rather than show them to be God. Judged from the point of view of intellectual definition, therefore, they are not God. But judged from the point of view of being the means by which these people could work as fully as their situation allows with God, they could be the best means available. And God, we have remembered, is the one who lives, and who is therefore known by us in the living with him rather than in conceiving of him intellectually.

It is no accident, therefore, that in Hinduism and Buddhism, as religions of escape from many of the personal aspects of life, there is no clear teaching about one God. Islam, with its acknowledged borrowings from the Old Testament and Christianity, is different. But it tends to deny a truly personal relationship (i.e., a partnership) between God and man: it is God who fixes a man's destiny, so that man must just stoically accept it. God may be a person, but not in our regard.

From all this I think the following results come. First, real contact with God is *life* with God. Second, this contact was given the name of contact with God(s) in pre-Christian religions, but this doesn't amount to belief in God in an intellectually valid sense. Third, in this post-Christian age, where non-Christians do not grow up with a tendency to think of the deepest level of their experience in terms of God—where alone he can be found—they would, of themselves, find that they believed in God only after careful and therefore rare reflection. Toward such a recognition the life and belief of the Church can and should help them. But obviously the opposite takes place if and when the God of the only religion they regularly meet has been falsely presented to them to have little real connection with our lives and personal values. This is also true of the Christian—especially of the younger generation —if God is falsely presented to them in worship, as we shall notice in a moment.

# IV
# The Christian
# Experience of God

In this post-Christian world we also have today's Christian (of which I am one), and we must finally ask about our belief in God and our attitude to that of non-Christians.

What has happened in the Jewish and Christian religions is that an assurance has been given that what one might, by careful reflection, have dared to suspect is implicit in life is true. The permanently unavoidable danger is, however, that instead we see them as the provider of special information about an almost private chief, so that they are to do with his private world rather than with life. In this view of it, God imparts supernatural grace to the soul which sustains us "in this vale of tears" as we move toward "another world." All these expressions are capable of saying true and useful things to us. But they have for many of us become so enmeshed with a picture of a God who is not at the radiantly creative center of life, that they can result in both a false apprehension of God and an impoverished kind of sharing in his work in the world.

But if the opportunity of this Christian assurance is really taken, it means that God, ourselves and the world are known as we are.

First it means that we know that the very pattern and texture of life *is* the finding of meaning: in other words, that the value of ourselves and of others move, in the very nature of things, toward fulfillment: "With those who love him, God turns everything to their good" (Rom. 8:28).

Since human life and love obviously rest on the appreciation of value, and since part of the perception of the value of anything is of its transiency (and hence of the liability to *non-value*), the assurance that there is a God should make of life an immensely rich *experience*. I don't just say an immensely rich *thing*—though it is that. But a rich *experience* because life is something that we do and feel ourselves doing. And if we merely know about the richness of life lived with God, as a theological doctrine to be stored in the corner of our mind reserved for it, then we haven't received the good news for what it is.

This richness is found, therefore, in the experience of joining in the creativity of God among people.

This is in fact only another way of putting the earliest definition of the Christian. This was expressed particularly at the moment of a man's entry into the Christian community in baptism. As he was being immersed, each was asked whether he believed in the Father, and in the Son, and in *the Spirit acting through the Church*. The Spirit, as we have seen, had long meant the creative presence of God. The function of the Church, therefore, was to be especially involved in the creativeness of personal value and significance—that is, the life of God.

We have seen that all people, by the very fact that they are people, are so involved, so we must ask what is special about the involvement of the Christian—insofar, of course, as we fulfill our vocation.

A Christian is someone who belongs to a community that is for all men: in other words, to help them find and live the full significance of a human life. This is because its vocation is to be the embodiment of Christ's presence today, and it was for this purpose that he came to us.

Since it is for all men, it should live with all men and should therefore be at the forefront in the development of human values.

It should do this in a full consciousness of its rich and personal significance. This will be fostered especially when particular communities come together for reflection and the Eucharist. In their reflection they will bring to articulateness what they are doing and mean to do for the world. For this reflection will be based on a consideration of the action of God in human lives, particularly as this has been at the very center of the experience of a whole people. And it will increase our awareness that we have a special part to play in that action: special because our activity is just that self-communication of God which is at the center of all that is most real.

If this reflection serves to open our eyes to the kind of opportunity we have been given, and if it makes us want to commit ourselves to it, then our natural reaction will be celebration. Celebration is the way that human beings say to life as they understand it: "Yes, that is how it *should* be; I'll come in fully on that." It is our assent to life.

It is this because it is a deliberate involvement in life in its wholeness (however dimly perceived), rather than in the small slabs of it that we restrict ourselves to for the convenience of ordinary living.[1]

In the light of this it is obvious why the Eucharist—that cry of wonder and thanks for the fact that life is filled with God and our commitment as a community to our part of this—should be the natural culmination of the reflection we have been discussing and a vital part in our coming to experience God.

This can only be so, of course, if the Eucharist really is the expression of a group that is willing to respond to that challenge. The consequences for the Christian experience of God, when the Eucharist is not like this, need therefore to be given very serious consideration.

We could end this chapter by considering how

[1] Cf. Harvey Cox, *The Feast of Fools*, 1969, pp. 21-26.

someone recently expressed these consequences. If he is right, the truer understanding of God that we have seen to be possible will not become widely available until we take a fresh look at what our worship is for: "By keeping just barely up with the times (in the way we worship), and reflecting only the mood people are presently in, we are always slightly behind the times and never truly contemporary. We do not lead the spirits of the worshipers, or challenge them. Consequently our ideas of God are usually more neat and precise than they ought to be. They are more comfortable than they have a right to be. People are not put upon to reach or stretch or reconceive anything. Their systems can handle things very well, and they go on subconsciously believing that God can really fit into the limited confines of their own existence. We are only catering further to the supreme inversion which has occurred in Western theological life sometime during the past millenium or two, whereby God depends upon man for his validity and not man upon God. It is no wonder, given the ways by which we try to worship God, that we have finally begun to suspect that he is dead, or just not up to the modern sense of reality."[2]

Openness to God is openness to the fullness of life. It involves, of its very nature, the courage to step out of the neat categories by which we become our own Gods (fashioning life under our own safe

[2] John Killinger, *Leave It to the Spirit,* 1971 p. 11.

administration) in order to live in the real world. It was to help all men to do this that Christ came. And the only purpose of the Church he founded is to join him in that.

# V

# Recent Ideas
# About God

In this book we have tried to do something very simple. First we considered what we mean by God. Then we tried to see what was the New Testament experience of God. And lastly we inquired what relevance this has to the experience of God in our civilization, both for Christian and non-Christian.

In this short discussion the aim has been to consider God in terms of our basic experience, our actual *living*. The reasons for this have been explained. As a consequence, refinement of the *concepts* used has taken second place to a hopefully accurate description of *experience*. But now that the overall picture has been sketched in, some more delicate etching could be useful. A useful way of doing this would be to compare the view offered in this book with that of other contemporary writers on the subject.

First of all, I took as my starting point the assertion that "God, if he exists, has supreme power, and is personal." This could be misleading on two counts. First it could look as though I were setting up a concept of God and then going on to try to prove that *it* exists. I agree with Leslie Dewart that this would be a mistaken undertaking, because "belief must bear *directly* upon the reality of God, not upon words or upon concepts . . . [for] God reveals himself, not words about or concepts of himself. . . . [We should] be concerned with showing how God himself *in his reality* is *present* to human experience."

But my starting point, though it may look like a definition, is simply a brief indication of what human experience, where alone we can find any God, really consists of: the personal.

I describe personal as sharing in the enjoyment and creation of meaning. This is based primarily on my experience of happy and unhappy marriages and is applicable to other personal experiences. Seen in terms of these, it need not seem too abstract. It is the same as love, for love is not a warm concern of some*thing static,* but of some*one* who has personality insofar as he aspires to be more himself *as such.* It is the same as goodness, which Thomas Aquinas magnificently defined as "something that of its very nature shares itself" (*bonum est diffusivum suiipsius*).

I was therefore simply stressing that God, if he exists, is found in the personal; and I said what I think the personal is. Hence there was no need at that point to take up the problem of what one means by calling God a person. The problem is that by person we mean today someone who is *finding* himself, and doing this partly by separating himself out from even the people he shares with. We must have "our own personality." I must be not you (however much I may like and admire you) but *myself,* and to be that must be to some extent fenced off from you.

But this is because we dare not, at present, risk being fully personal. Or one can put this another way by saying that in the personal, which is the highest kind of reality we know, we experience an ideal of a total self-communication which transcends our present powers. But because it is at least glimpsed as an ideal we perhaps realize that total self-communication would be total possession of oneself, and that *is,* even for us, an ideal: something to which we have aspiration.

Or we could express it by saying that we know that our personality is, like a field, or capital, or like those talents Christ spoke of, not for safekeeping in a strongbox but for personal integration with other persons. This is what personality, as we experience it, consists of.

But this quest for integration points toward a finding. In fact it is a *reasonable* quest only insofar as full integration is possible. And therefore we know that we experience only part of the possibilities of being a person.

And in fact what Christ came to tell us, as we

have seen, was that the life both of God and of ourselves *is* greater than our experience of being a person. The life of God, he showed us, while certainly the life of total fulfillment that we conceive it to be, is one where this fulfillment is found not in isolated possession but in personal and "creative" self-communication. Christ did not come primarily to say to us: you thought there was just *one* God, while in fact there are three. He was not concerned with numbers but with life: the life of God in which we share. And everything about him—not merely what he said, but still more what he was and did— was evidence that this life consisted of self-communication.

One of the clearest instances of this is the fifth chapter of St. John, where the power and work of Christ is seen simply as the full sharing in the Father's action and presence. But far more important than the collection of instances is the perception that *all* Christ meant was that life does consist in being a person through self-communication; that the fullness of living is therefore where this is achieved; that life is like this in fact because all human life is some kind of involvement in the fullness of living; and that he had come to offer that life "more abundantly." He bore this out by founding a group of people (the Church) whose job consists of communicating to others a possibility of a greater involvement in this.

As everyone is aware, the last ten years have been a period when much thought has been given by Christians to a truer understanding of God. Books have proliferated on the subject. New about these books is that several of them have been written at quite a popular level and have had correspondingly "popular" titles. From all this labor, no very clear picture has yet emerged.

All this was certainly to be expected. What we have seen happening in these ten years is this.

First there was the application to the problem of understanding God of new insights that had long been increasingly taken for granted in human affairs. And second there was the increasingly explicit consciousness of a great number of Christians that their understanding or picture of God did not correspond with these new insights and that therefore what *claims* to be most real was in fact for them unreal.

All this surged onto the popular stage in the 1960's, and clear vision of the course it was taking was not made easier by a persistent talk of "the death of God" (a gift title, of course, for the mass publisher) when the apparent assertion of atheism wasn't in fact intended.[1]

But neither the complexity nor the stridency of the debate should be allowed to blind us to the value of these gropings toward truth. And the leaning toward paradox, as in the "death of God" phrase itself, often stems from an anguished recognition that for vast numbers of Western people belief in the God we knew no longer seems a real option.

A full survey of this new thought about God

cannot be offered here. But it might be useful to comment on how some of the valuable contributions it has made blend with the perspectives suggested in this book. I hope that, by taking two fairly typical examples, evidence will be given that this kind of thought has much to offer.

My first example will be Schubert M. Ogden, Professor of Divinity at Chicago.

Ogden's first main contention is that, for modern man especially, belief in God is unavoidable. Modern man, he reminds us, does not look for explanations *outside* life, in some supernatural superstructure. He has rejected all that. Instead his attention is directed to reality as we actually meet it, such as the intricate interconnections of physical things (the world of science) or the demands of moral choice.

Now it is precisely in *that* world, he says, that we can find God—and, in fact, only in that world. This is because we find in that world something that reassures us of the significance of life. And it is just this reassurance that we mean when we talk of God. " 'God' is the very meaning of 'reality' when this word is defined in terms of our basic confidence in the significance of life."[2]

This may well strike us as a somewhat strange understanding of God in some respects. But before

[1] Cf. Alistair Kee, *The Way of Transcendence*, 1971, pp. 65-112.
[2] *The Reality of God*, 1967, p. 39.

coming to that, it is important to do justice to the very solid basis on which Ogden builds it.

For it simply is true that our moral decisions, for instance, are based on an assurance that life has meaning. In fact we take it for granted that a person's humanity be judged not by the *correctness* of his evaluation of life's meaning (however important) but by the courage and sincerity of his response to it—in other words, by his seeking for the meaning of life.

So Ogden, we see, looks for God within our experience of life—and where else could we find the life-ful? Also he rightly asserts that many people regard themselves as atheists because the "God" offered them for belief is manifestly a self-contradiction: a life-less supernatural construct, inhabiting a remote, self-sufficient world, yet claiming to be the center of life.

All these, I suggest, are useful assertions. First they direct us to the obvious truth that if there is a God he can be known, not through intellectual acknowledgment of some other world, but at the center of whatever life we experience. And second they do remind us of our perception of an ultimate value in our lives, however fitfully and obscurely we may glimpse it.

The chief question that must be faced, though, is whether Ogden has found in our experience of reality what we could meaningfully call "God." Can what he has found in it be called personal? When he says, for instance: "I hold the primary use or function of 'God' is to refer to the objective ground in reality itself of our ineradicable confidence in the final worth of our existence,"[3] is that "objective ground" personal?

Well of course the phrase hasn't about it a personal ring. And at first sight the difficulty is increased by the fact that it is not initially clear whether "objective ground" and "reality itself" are meant as identical. But although his critics haven't always observed this,[4] he clearly states his position: "To speak of a ground of significance or worth except as involving . . . relatedness is logically impossible. . . . Of necessity, therefore, the ground of the significance of our life has to be a supremely relative reality. God must enjoy real internal relations to all our actions and so be affected by them in his own actual being."[5]

The main limitation of Ogden's essay seems to me to arise not from the inconsistency of some of its statements (no genuine statement about God can avoid that) but from the kind of essay it is: one based on philosophical argument rather than on Scripture. The limitation of a philosophical essay on God is that, however elucidating to the mind, it tends

[3] Ibid., p. 37.

[4] E.g., Alistair Kee, who seems to have omitted page 47 in his reading of Ogden's book (*The Way of Transcendence*, 1971, pp. 40-42).

[5] *The Reality of God*, p. 47.

to leave important reaches of our personality disengaged. And God, as Ogden sees, is above all the one who engages us as persons.

For what it seeks to be, the essay certainly has great value. Particularly valuable is his explanation of the viewpoint that reality should be seen not in terms of static "substances" but in terms of the self, which is relational and social. His conclusion is that "God is now conceived as precisely the unique or in all ways perfect instance of creative becoming" and that "he is understood to be continually in process of self-creation, synthesizing in each now moment of his experience the whole of achieved actuality with the plentitude of possibility as yet unrealized."[6]

I think that such statements do usefully direct our *minds* toward a better understanding of God, and I am not sure that "creative becoming" need, when looked at carefully, imply incompleteness in God. In terms of what it seeks to be, therefore, a "theology aspiring to an adequacy always beyond its grasp,"[7] I suggest that Ogden's essay is most helpful.

The limitation of any such theological inquiry is that personality in God can, if found at all, only be *deduced*. From an important point of view this is not a limitation but a strength: it reminds us of what one can so easily neglect that reality can only

6 Ibid., p. 59.
7 Ibid., p. 56.

really be understood in terms of the personal. But from the other point of view it means that what is there to astonish and win us by its presence can appear as abstract or remote.

The Christian God, at least, is not merely to be known about and understood, but to be loved: to be delighted in as the person in our midst. Books like Ogden's can inform our minds of how deeply in our midst God is, and that he must have the personal qualities of relatedness and so on. But though our minds help us to know persons better, they are not by themselves alone the means by which we encounter people. Other faculties are needed to convey to us their actuality and warmth. There is a here-and-now-ness about persons as we come to know them that no concept can catch.

That is one reason why, in my opinion, valuable approaches like Ogden's need to be complemented by the Christian revelation of God in Christ.

But I think there is another. For we need to feel ourselves involved not merely in the concrete actuality of "the full expression" of God but also of his all-embracing concern. Particularly perhaps today, man needs from God support. This need not come from a callow fear of life. It may instead arise from the very natural perception that life is very vulnerable and fleeting, and that alone and inevitably we die. The senselessness about this transiency dismays our minds and our emotions. To this dismay the great images of the Bible (themselves the expression of the growing consciousness of a whole people) of God as shepherd, rock, husband, and father speak more deeply than could any concept.

My second example is John Robinson, who as the Bishop of Woolwich published his *Honest to God* in March 1963 and had sold a quarter of a million copies in just four weeks. Since the book made no pretense of being either original or particularly easy-reading, it obviously had something in it which many people wanted to hear.

The purpose of this book was not primarily to compose a new definition of God but to show people living in our modern scientific age where God may be found. In order to attempt this, Robinson had to warn his readers that the quest for God was not as it had often been presented in the past: a turning away from the world toward "a Person who looks down at this world which he has made and loves from 'out there.' "[8] Instead God "is to be found only in, with *and under* the conditioned relationships of this life: for his *is* their depth and ultimate significance."[9] We can find God, in other words, only in our relationships with our fellow human beings.

The value of Robinson's book is in its assertion that human experience—at its deepest, most personal, and most real—is where alone we can know God. This value, and the attractiveness of the book, are considerably increased by the honesty rightly

[8] *Honest to God,* 1963, p. 30.
[9] *Ibid.,* p. 60.

claimed in the book's title. Here is a man, we feel, who is doing his best to help his contemporaries find what they have lost, and who is doing this with considerable diffidence but in terms of his own wrestling with the problem. The quest for any person, whether for God or not, must in the last resort be for us as individual persons. And in presenting it in this way he reminds us of an important truth about God.

It would be unfortunate if we were to be deflected from profiting from the book's merits by too great a concentration on its defects. But it could mislead us if they are not faced.

Although excellent on the question of where God may be found, Robinson is less helpful on what he is. The reason for this is that he neglects the fact that the effects of our personal actions (such as the way we bring up our families) show us not merely what we have done but also *something of what we are*. The consequence is that, although the book often deals impressively with our experience as a manifestation of God's presence and "quality," the personality that exercises that "quality" recedes.

To put the matter more technically, his limitation is "an insufficient advertence to the fact that in the revelation through salvation history the absolute meaning of God communicates itself to our faith even though we can then express the reality of this datum only indirectly."[10]

[10] E. Schillebeeckx, *God and Man*, 1969, p. 153.

# Conclusion

A book about God is a clumsy thing. Like any person he is better known in living. The best "description" of God is the community of people, the Church, in the way of life it partly lives and partly aspires to.

All a book can do is to help clarify our outlook. And there are various reasons why this is particularly worth doing today.

First, we are better able today to appreciate the personal—and it is the application of this insight, as it affects the lives of people I know, that has been the main point of this book. And, second, we have been aware, through the research of scholars, of the reality and significance of Jesus' life.

The point of Christianity is to offer evidence, through the life of people, that God is personally among us. If this book has done anything to throw light on the *relevance* of that evidence to our hopes and fears, our happiness and our sufferings, then it will have been worthwhile.